Cardcaptor
Sakura
CLEAR CARD

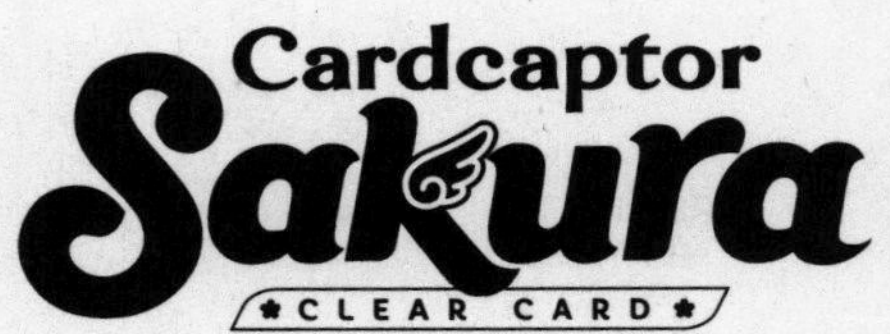
Cardcaptor
Sakura
CLEAR CARD

CLAMP

3

Cardcaptor Sakura

CLEAR CARD

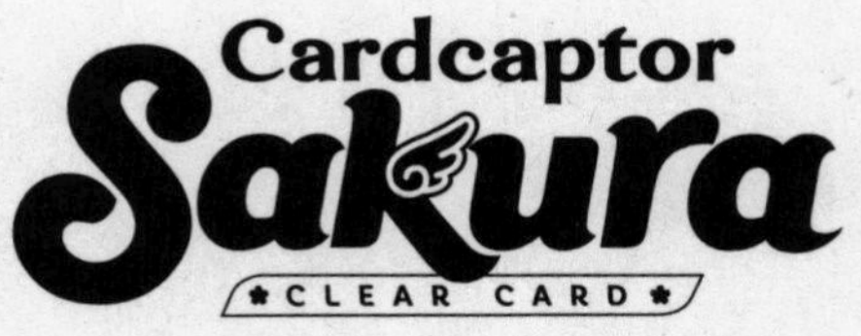
Cardcaptor
Sakura
CLEAR CARD

A FLOWER-VIEWING PARTY IS A JAPANESE TRADITION WELCOMING THE SPRING. FRIENDS GATHER OUTDOORS AND HOLD AN ALL-DAY PICNIC AMONG THE FLOWERING TREES. THE SAKURA BLOSSOM SEASON IN TOMOEDA WOULD BE IN EARLY APRIL.

...ESPECIALLY BECAUSE SYAORAN-KUN WAS THERE!

POP
MUSTA BEEN NICE... MUSTA BEEN SO NICE... A FLOWER-VIEWING PARTY...
I WISH I COULDA BEEN THERE, TOO!
IF IT WAS JUST ME, TOMOYO-CHAN, AND SYAORAN-KUN, IT WOULD HAVE BEEN FINE...
Sorry.
WELL, I GUESS YOU BROUGHT ME SOME SNACKS BACK, SO I'LL FORGIVE YOU THIS ONCE.
OH, HEY, YOU SAID THAT ONE TRANSFER STUDENT WAS THERE?
YEAH!
AKIHO-CHAN!
THE SNACKS I GAVE YOU WERE ORIGINALLY FROM HER.
PUMP!
AW YEAH! SHE'S A KEEPER!

YEAH!
SHE'S REALLY SUPER NICE!
AND, YOU KNOW WHAT? SHE EVEN SANG WITH TOMOYO-CHAN AT THE PARTY!
CLAP
CLAP
CLAP
CLAP
AS GOOD AS EVER, TOMOYO-CHAN!
CLAP
CLAP
CLAP
CLAP
CLAP
I THOUGHT AKIHO-CHAN WAS QUITE LOVELY, MY-SELF.
THANK YOU VERY MUCH!
YES!
THAT WAS GREAT!

WHAT'S THAT?
I HEARD YOU HUMMING ALONG WHILE I WAS SINGING.
YOU HAVE QUITE THE LOVELY SINGING VOICE!
FLAIL FLAIL FLAIL
わたわたわた
OH, I AM SO SORRY! I DID NOT MEAN TO BOTHER YOU.
NOT AT ALL! I WAS GLAD.
WOULD YOU CARE TO SING A DUET?

FWUBBLE
はわ
B-
BUT...
I'VE
NEVER SUNG
IN FRONT OF
OTHER PEO-
PLE BEFORE!
I MIGHT
NOT BE ANY
GOOD AT IT...
FWUB-UBBLE
はわわ
TURN
くりん!
Hey!
I WANT
TO
HEAR
YOU
SING!
PLEASE!
SING
FOR US!
HOP
I—
I'LL TRY!
CLAP
ぱち
CLAP
ぱち
CLAP
ぱち

DO YOU KNOW THIS TUNE, AKIHO-CHAN?
I DO! WE LEARNED THIS SONG WHEN I WAS FIRST STUDYING JAPANESE.
IT IS MY FAVORITE!
INHALE

WHAT'D THEY SING?
SHKSHHH
"MISTY MOON"!
♪ THE SUN FADES AWAY INTO THE FIELD OF CANOLA BLOSSOMS… ♪
OH, HEY!
I KNOW THAT ONE! A CLASSIC SPRINGTIME SONG!
TOMOYO-CHAN AND AKIHO-CHAN WERE BOTH WONDERFUL!
I WISH I COULD HAVE RECORDED IT…
YOU HAD YOUR PHONE, RIGHT?
I ONLY THOUGHT OF THAT AFTER.
I WISH I COULD JUST THINK, "NOW!"
AND HAVE IT BE RECORDED RIGHT INTO MY MEMORY.

SHABING!
IF YOU COULD DO THAT, YOU'D NEVER HAVE AN EXCUSE TO MISS CAPTURING MY HANDSOME MUG!
WELL, DON'T YOU HAVE A CELL PHONE TOO, KERO-CHAN? TOMOYO-CHAN GAVE YOU ONE.
FWAP
YEP!
ISN'T TOMOYO-CHAN'S MOM'S COMPANY GREAT?
THEY MAKE ALL KINDS OF STUFF NOW! ELECTRONICS AND COMPUTERS-NOT JUST TOYS ANYMORE!
THEY MADE MY CUSTOM GAMING HEADSET, TOO!
KSHHH
YEAH, YOU'RE ALWAYS GAMING ONLINE WITH THAT THING!
I'LL BEAT THAT SPINNY NEXT TIME, WATCH ME!
UH-OH!
SLIDE

OH!
AKIHO-CHAN!
SHE'S THAT TRANSFER STUDENT YOU TALKED ABOUT?
YEAH!
"SPEAK OF THE DEVIL..."
...AIN'T IT?
AKIHO-CHAN!
SKREEK
SAKURA-SAN!

GOOD AFTER-NOON!
HELLO!
ARE YOU OUT RUNNING ERRANDS?
YEP! I'M BUYING STUFF FOR DINNER TONIGHT.
WHAT ABOUT YOU?
I AM SHOP-PING AS WELL.
BUT I JUST MOVED HERE, SO I DON'T KNOW WHERE THE GOOD SHOPS ARE...
WHY DON'T YOU COME WITH ME?
I CAN SHOW YOU AROUND!
OH, THANK YOU!
SHOOOSH
SPEAKING OF, THE BOXED LUNCH WE HAD AT THE FLOWER-VIEWING PARTY...
IT WAS SO NICE AND NEAT, AND REALLY TASTY, TOO.
DID YOU MAKE THAT ALL BY YOURSELF, AKIHO-CHAN?

WHOA!
お おおー
KA-DING!
ペカー
NO, NO! SOMEONE MADE IT FOR ME.
I AM VERY CLUMSY. I COULD NEVER!
DID YOU COME TO JAPAN WITH THE PERSON WHO MADE IT?
NOD
こくこくこく
NOD
NOD
YES.
HE'S SOMEONE WHO HAS LOOKED AFTER ME SINCE I WAS LITTLE.
FAMILY?
NO...
WE ARE NOT RELATED, BUT...

HE IS VERY SPECIAL TO ME.
YOU MUST LOVE HIM VERY MUCH.
WHAT ?!
YOU HAD SUCH A LOVING LOOK ON YOUR FACE.
WHAT ?!
WHAT ?!

OH!
THAT BUNNY!
IT'S SO CUTE!
WE ARE ALWAYS TOGETHER.
BUT I WASN'T SURE IF I COULD BRING HER TO SCHOOL...
I TOOK HER WITH ME TO THE FLOWER-VIEWING PARTY, BUT I THOUGHT I MIGHT SEEM TOO CHILDISH IF I HAD HER OUT...
NOT AT ALL!
THERE'S NO RULE AGAINST IT AT SCHOOL. I'M SURE EVERYONE WOULD THINK IT'S REALLY CUTE!
KSHHH
すぃ
TIP TAP TIP
てこてこてこ

I ALWAYS HAVE KERO-CH-
UM!
はっ!
...A STUFFED ANIMAL NAMED KERO-CHAN WITH ME! HE'S VERY IMPORTANT TO ME.
...
JUST LIKE ME, THEN!
YEAH!
FLAP
わた
FLAP
わた
FLAP
わた
I WILL BRING HER TO SCHOOL TOMORROW, THEN!
HUG
きゅ
AND YOU, SAKURA-SAN?
GLANCE
ちら...
UM...
I WILL...

THUMBS UP
FLASH
ぱっ
I'LL BRING KERO-CHAN!
SHINE
ぱあっ
DOES SHE HAVE A NAME?
YES!
HER NAME IS MOMO.

I'M SAKURA!
NICE TO MEET YOU, MOMO-CHAN!
HAND-SHAKE
あくしゅ あくしゅ
I'M SURE YOU'LL BE GOOD FRIENDS!
RIGHT, MOMO?
I LOVE MAKING NEW FRIENDS!
LIFE IS A LOT BUSIER NOW, BUT IT'S GREAT FUN EVERY DAY!
I'M HOME!

WELCOME HOME,
SAKURA-SAN.
YOU'RE HOME!
WHAT ABOUT WORK?
I WON'T BE ABLE TO STAY OVER-NIGHT FOR A WHILE...
...BUT I NEEDED SOME RESEARCH MATERIALS FROM HOME.
Oh, I see!
CLINK
I'M HOME, MOM!
...

WHAT'S WRONG?
IT'S NOTHING.
WERE YOU OUT SHOPPING?
YEAH! IT'S MY TURN TO MAKE DINNER TONIGHT!
YOU'RE MAKING POTATO GRATIN TONIGHT?
YOU GOT IT!
AND...
OMELETTES?
PERHAPS?
THOSE ARE FOR LUNCH.
I WANT TO TRY TO MAKE BETTER LUNCHES.

Fujitaka
Back home soon? Text me.
Toya
Work after school
be home for dinn
Sakura
Back by 4!
I'm going sho
IT SAYS HERE THAT YOU WERE SUPPOSED TO BE HOME EARLIER...
I'M SORRY I WAS LATE!
NO NEED TO APOLOGIZE, I DON'T MIND.
DID YOU STOP SOME-WHERE?
I MET A FRIEND! WE WENT SHOPPING TOGETHER.
THE TRANSFER STUDENT I TOLD YOU ABOUT!
OH, THE ONE WHO HAD LIVED ALL OVER THE WORLD?
SHE'S REALLY SUPER NICE, AND CUTE, TOO!
ポーン♪
DIIING
さっ
FWIP
IT'S BIG BRO!
IT'S TOYA-KUN.

HE'S ASKING IF TSUKISHIRO-KUN CAN COME OVER FOR DINNER.
OF COURSE HE CAN!
I'LL DO MY BEST COOKING!
SMILE
THIS IS GREAT!
I'M SO GLAD!
GLARE
WELL, IT'S ALL RIGHT.
MUNCH MUNCH
むぐむぐ

WHAT ABOUT FUJITAKA-SAN?
HE ATE ALREADY AND THEN WENT BACK TO SCHOOL.
HE'S SO BUSY THESE DAYS.
UM... YUKITO-SAN?
WHAT IS IT?
HOW IS YOUR APPETITE?
HUH? I'M EATING ALL THIS DELICIOUS FOOD RIGHT NOW...
NO, I MEAN...
IS IT ENOUGH? ARE YOU SATISFIED?
ARE YOU STILL HUNGRY?
NO, I'M OKAY.
I DON'T GET AS HUNGRY AS I USED TO.
TILT
YOU STILL EAT ENOUGH FOR TWO, THOUGH.

BEFORE, YUKITO-SAN HAD TO EAT A WHOLE LOT TO MAKE UP FOR MY LACK OF MAGICAL POWER.
HE'S OKAY NOW, SO I HOPE THIS THING WITH THE NEW CARDS ISN'T TROUBLING YUKITO-SAN OR YUE-SAN...
OH!
A ROOKIE MISTAKE.
FWIP
WHAAAA?!

SHIIING
SHIIING
?!
JUMP

SHIIIING

ARE YOU...
...TRYING TO TELL ME SOMETHING?
THE KEY?
YOU WANT THE KEY?

To be continued...

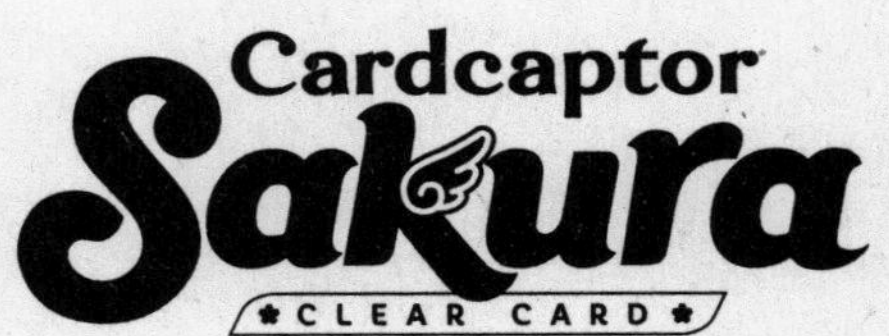
Cardcaptor
Sakura
CLEAR CARD

Cardcaptor
Sakura
CLEAR CARD

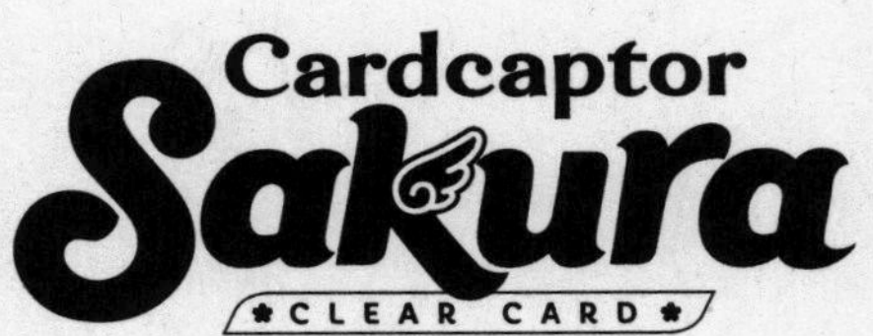
Cardcaptor
Sakura
CLEAR CARD

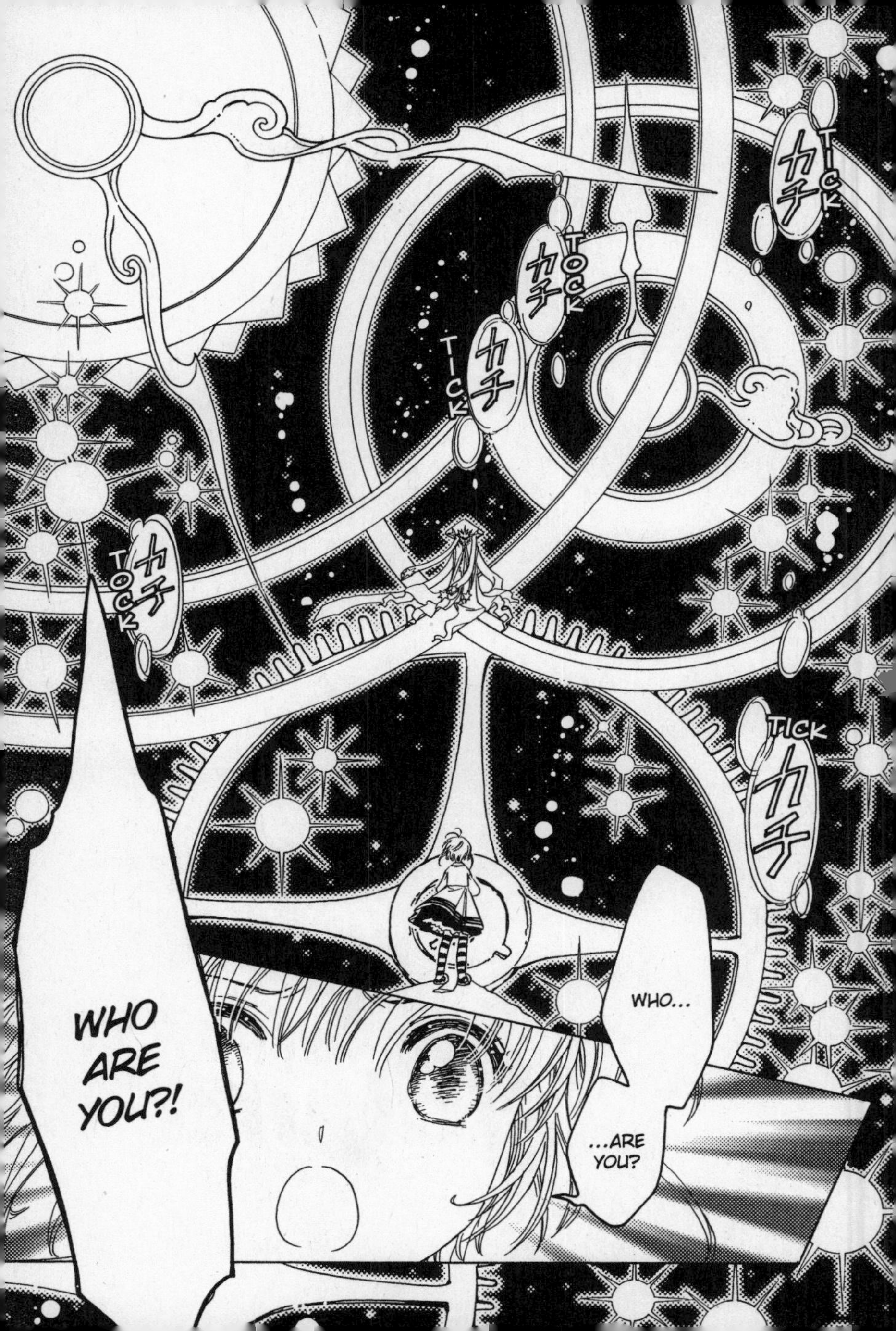
カチ TICK
カチ TOCK
カチ TICK
カチ TOCK
カチ TICK
WHO...
...ARE YOU?
WHO ARE YOU?!

SAKURA-CHAN?
GASP
... HUH?
ARE YOU OKAY?
FLUSTER あわ
FLUSTER あわ
DID I...
...FALL ASLEEP?

NO, BUT...
YOU DIDN'T RESPOND WHEN WE SPOKE TO YOU.
SORRY FOR SPACING OUT LIKE THAT.
CLATTER
がた…
OH, RIGHT!
I HAVE SOME REALLY GOOD BREAD, TOO!
STIP STIP
ぱたぱた
...

TWEEDLE-DEET
MORNING!
GOOD MORNING!
POP
HIYA!
OH, KERO-CHAN!
I PROMISED AKIHO-CHAN I'D BRING HIM.
AKIHO-CHAN?

AH, SO THAT'S WHY YOU BROUGHT HIM!
KERO-CHAN IS ACTUALLY PRETTY BIG.
HE WOULD STAND OUT TOO MUCH OUTSIDE MY BAG.
MUTTER
ぶちぶち
MUTTER
Y'KNOW, I GET THAT.
SLIM
ちょこん
BUT I AIN'T SO SURE ABOUT THIS.
I'M NOT REALLY SURE A CHARM BIGGER THAN THE PHONE ITSELF IS THAT GOOD, EITHER.
Hmm...
IT'S VERY CUTE.
FLASH
ぱっ
YOU THINK?!
WHAT A SIMPLE CREATURE...

OH, YOU BROUGHT TWO BAGS WITH YOU TODAY, TOMOYO-CHAN?
We don't have gym today, do we?!
SHOULD AN OPPORTUNITY TO RECORD YOU EVER ARISE, I NEED TO BE PREPARED! THAT'S WHY I'M CARRYING A COSTUME WITH ME WHEREVER I GO!
FLUTTER
POP
Nice!
JUST MAKE SURE YOU HAVE A COOL ONE FOR ME, TOO!
WHAAAA ?!

I want one with a crown next time!
Oh, that would be just lovely! And Sakura-chan's would have a tiara...
きゃっ
CHATTER
きゃっ
CHATTER
TWEEDLE-DEET
ピピピ...
WHAT NICE WEATHER...
I WISH I COULD RECORD THIS, TOO.
WHIRR

"WHIRR?"

WHA?

WHAT WAS THAT SOUND?

HEY!

WE ALL RIGHT ON TIME?

MIGHT WANNA GET A MOVE ON!

ACK!

WE BETTER HURRY!

LET'S GO, TOMOYO-CHAN!

DASH

"IS THIS SHIP HEADED WEST?"

A DUBIOUS LOOK PASSED ACROSS THE BOATMAN'S FACE, AND HE LOOKED AT ME ASKANCE.

FINALLY, HE REPLIED IN A SINGLE WORD: "WHY?"

"IT SEEMS WE ARE FOLLOWING AFTER THE SETTING SUN."

THAT'S ENOUGH.

THANK YOU, KINOMOTO-SAN.

CLATTER かたん

WHEW ほっ

TEN NIGHTS OF DREAMS COLLECTS STORIES OF UNSETTLING DREAMS LIKE THIS ONE.

EACH STORY IS FICTION, AND OFTEN FANTASTICAL, BUT DESPITE THE UNREALITY OF IT, THE SUBJECT MATTER IS OFTEN QUITE SCARY.

NOW,
THERE ARE ALSO WHAT ARE CALLED "PROPHETIC DREAMS."
DO YOU KNOW ABOUT THEM?
THIS KIND OF DREAM IS ABOUT THE FUTURE.
THE DREAMS IN *TEN NIGHTS OF DREAMS* AREN'T PROPHETIC, BUT...
...THROUGH DREAM INTERPRETA-TION...
PROPHETIC DREAMS...
I WONDER IF THAT DREAM IS ONE?

I DREAMED ABOUT BOTH KAHO-SENSEI AND ERIOL-KUN BEFORE MEETING THEM, TOO.
LET'S CONTINUE.
SHINO-MOTO-SAN?
PING
HUH?!
YOU CAN DO IT, AKIHO-CHAN!
Um...
er...
Go for it!
TURN

YOU
FLAP ぱく
CAN
FLAP ぱく
FLAP ぱく
DO
FLAP ぱく
IT!
TREMBLE ぷるぷる… TREMBLE
GULP ごくっ
BREATHE すう
"WHEN I LOOKED TOWARDS THE BOW...
...I SAW A GREAT MANY SAILORS THERE, HOISTING THE HALYARD.
I
I BECAME QUITE DISHEART-ENED.
I DID NOT KNOW WHEN WE WOULD NEXT SIGHT LAND.
NOR DID I KNOW WHERE WE WERE GOING.
DING カ
DOOONG コーン
DAAAANG キーン

I'm starving!
Where should we eat?
わい
CHATTER
わい
CHATTER
YOUR READING WAS GREAT!
I HOPE I MANAGED TO READ IT WELL ENOUGH.
IT WAS QUITE WON-DERFUL!
NOD
NOD
NOD
whew
OH, HEY! AKIHO-CHAN, HAVE YOU THOUGHT ABOUT A SCHOOL CLUB?
I'M STILL DECIDING...

OH!
あ
WHAT ABOUT THE CHORAL ENSEMBLE?
YOU DON'T THINK I WOULD BE IN THE WAY?
WE WOULD ALL LOVE TO HAVE YOU.
YES!
YOU WERE SO GOOD AT THE FLOWER-VIEWING PARTY!

きゅっ
SQUEEZE
...VERY WELL.
I WILL JOIN THE CHORAL ENSEMBLE!
YEAH!

EVERYONE'S SMILES ARE SO LOVELY...
WHIRR
HUH?
GLANCE
きょろ
That sound again!
きょろ
GLANCE

For today's lunch...
Okay, let's go!
Okay!
LI-KUN!
STEP
WHAT IS IT?
I'M GLAD TO SEE YOU.
I HAVE A FAVOR TO ASK OF YOU.

YES!
SHHP!
YOU'VE MATURED.
HAVE I?
YOU'RE QUITE THE ROBUST YOUNG MAN.
BLUSH
OH.
UM...
WHY DID YOU NEED MY MEA-SUREMENTS, TOO?
WHY, I WOULD LIKE TO MAKE COSTUMES FOR YOU TO WEAR, OF COURSE!
Eh heh heh

I WANT TO DO MY PART...
...TO MAKE BOTH OF YOU LOOK YOUR BEST!
HUH?
FLUTTER
WHAT WAS THAT JUST NOW?
GLANCE
きょろ
GLANCE
きょろ
THE WIND?

FLUTTER
THAT WAS ...!
THAT'S NO ORDINARY WIND.
I SAW SOMETHING.
LIKE THE EDGE OF A CLOTH FLUTTERING BY...
FLUTTER
CLAP
SHIIIING

WHAT ?!
VOOOOM
Raitei Shourai !
CRACKLE
CRACKLE
WHEN THE HECK DID YOU LEARN TO DO THAT?!
小僧の
YOU'RE JUST
くせに！
A KID!

SLIP
CRACKLE
SHIIING
IT'S GETTING AWAY!
WAIT!
CRACKLE
IF WE ATTACK IT, IT WILL TRY TO RUN...
FLUTTER
WHIRR
BUT...

IS IT JUST WIND?
I COULD USE "GALE"...
NO. IT WOULD NOTICE ME.
BUT IF I USED "SIEGE"...
GALE
SIEGE
NO.
NO MATTER WHAT HAPPENS TO ME, DON'T MOVE.
...

FLUTTER
I DON'T NEED TO CAPTURE IT BY FORCE.
I SHOULD DO...
...SOME-THING...
...A BIT MORE...
FLIT
WOULD YOU...
...LIKE TO BE FRIENDS?

OH!
CLATTER
WHIRR
THANK YOU.

FLUTTER

HEY!
YOU'RE FLYIN'!
IT'S GREAT!
I CAN MOVE SO EASILY!
TWIRL
WHIRR...
!
HM?
How wonderful!
Secure!
WHIRR...
WHIRR..
CRICK
CRACK

FLASH
TWINKLE
キラ
TWINKLE
キラ
キラ
TWINKLE
記録
THE NOISE WAS FROM THIS CARD!

FLUTTER
DRIFT
Secure!

FLASH
FLASH
FLIGHT
THE FLYING CARD THIS TIME IS A RIBBON, HUH?
I'M SURE THESE WILL COME IN HANDY!
To be continued...

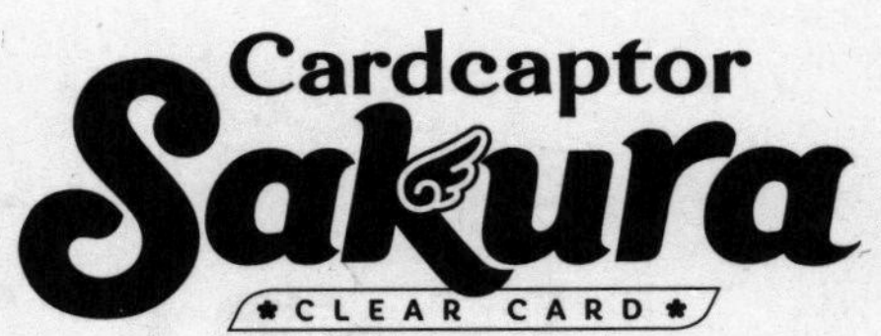
Cardcaptor
Sakura
CLEAR CARD

Cardcaptor
Sakura
CLEAR CARD

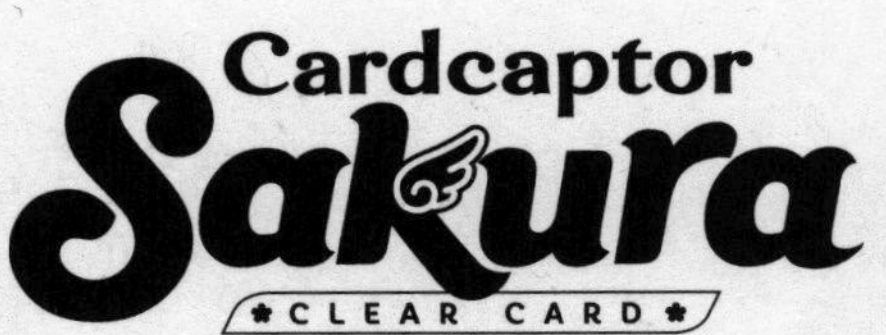
Cardcaptor
Sakura
CLEAR CARD

YOU'VE SEALED ANOTHER NEW CARD?
THAT'S RIGHT.
WE FOUND IT AT TOMOYO-CHAN'S HOUSE.
WHAT MANNER OF CARD IS IT?
HERE.
記録
RECORD
"RECORD" ...
LEAN
...YOU NEED NOT APPROACH THE SCREEN SO. I CAN SEE YOU.
WELL, I JUST FIGURED A CLOSE-UP WOULD MAKE YOU FEEL LIKE YOU'RE REALLY HERE!
WHAT CAN IT DO?

I HAVEN'T TRIED IT OUT YET.
I GET THE FEELING IT CAN MEMORIZE THINGS FOR LATER...
Awright!
LET'S TRY 'ER OUT!
YEAH!
Record!
FLASH
POIT

NOT MOVIN', HUH?
N- NO.
YOU PROLLY GOTTA ORDER IT TO DO STUFF, THEN.
Record a circle around me!
FLIT
FLIT
FLIT
FLIT
STOP
...DID IT RECORD IT?
Hmm...
I DON'T KNOW HOW TO PLAY IT BACK...

Show me what you have recorded!
FOOOSH
TURN
OOOOH!
IT'S LIKE I'M REALLY STANDING THERE!
SO THAT'S HOW YOU USE IT!
YOU SHOULD HAVE IT TAPE YUE!
I'LL PASS.

AT THE VERY LEAST, THERE SEEM TO BE NO ILL EFFECTS.
YEP.
IT SEEMS PRETTY USEFUL.
WHENEVER I WANT TO SAVE SOMETHING I CAN LET IT RECORD.
RECORD
I WAS JUST THINKING ABOUT HOW I'D LIKE TO BE ABLE TO DO THIS!
OH!
I HAVE TO GET GOING!
BYE, YUE-SAN!
TAKE CARE.
I WILL!
STP
STP

I'M HEADING OUT!
TAP
TIP
TAP
たたたっ
WUMPH
ぼふっ
AKIHO-CHAN!
GOOD MORNING!
MORNING!
AND GOOD MORNING TO YOU, MOMO-CHAN!

PLUSHIE MODE
Oh!
AND YOUR LITTLE FRIEND?
RUMMAGE
ごそごそ
RUMMAGE
GRAB
I DID BRING KERO-CHAN WITH ME TODAY!
HERE!
URK!
DANGLE
GOOD MORNING TO YOU, KERO-SAN!
CAN'T... BREATHE...! MY NECK...!!
Ah!
FREEZE
STUFF
BY THE WAY, WHERE-ABOUTS DO YOU LIVE, AKIHO-CHAN?
WHEEZE
HUFF
HUFF

IT'S CLOSE ENOUGH THAT I CAN WALK.
IT'S A SEPA-RATE BUILDING.
THERE WAS AN ENGLISH EXCHANGE STUDENT ABOUT MY AGE LIVING THERE BEFORE ME, I HEARD.
HUH ?!
DO YOU HAPPEN TO HAVE A PICTURE OF IT?
OH! YES.
BIP
ピ
ピ
BIP

THAT'S ERIOL-KUN'S PLACE!
HUH?!
FLUMP
I COULDN'T BREATHE ...
I ALMOST THOUGHT I WAS GOING TO KICK THE BUCKET...
OH... I'M SORRY ...
YOU BETTER TREAT ME A WHOLE LOT NICER FROM NOW ON!
ANYWAY, ABOUT THIS MORNIN'...
YEAH! AKIHO-CHAN'S HOUSE!
SHE LIVES WHERE HASEGAWA DID, RIGHT?

IT SURPRISED ME!
WHEN I TOLD AKIHO-CHAN THAT A FRIEND OF MINE USED TO LIVE THERE, SHE WAS SURPRISED TOO!
PREVIOUS OWNER
元家主です
SO THEN,
SHE ASKED IF WE WANTED TO COME OVER NEXT SUNDAY!
TO THE HOUSE IN QUESTION?
YEAH!
SHE WANTED TO SHOW ME THE BOOKS SHE'S COLLECTED FROM ALL THE COUNTRIES SHE'S VISITED.
MOST OF THEM ARE IN LANGUAGES I CAN'T READ...
...BUT SHE SAID THERE ARE ONES WITH PICTURES AND PHOTOGRAPHS, TOO!
SORRY... I'D COME WITH YOU, BUT I'M BUSY THAT DAY.
AWW, THAT'S TOO BAD.
IT'LL BE JUST ME AND TOMOYO-CHAN, THEN.
CAN YOU APOLOGIZE TO HER FOR ME?
I WILL.
OH, UM, HEY...
ARE YOU FREE THE SUNDAY AFTER NEXT?

I'VE, UM, BEEN TRYING TO MAKE REALLY GOOD OMELETTES ...
IT'S GETTING WARMER, SO IF THE WEATHER'S NICE, WE COULD GO OUT SOMEWHERE...
かあああ
BLUSH
IF YOU'D LIKE TO HAVE ME...
OF-OF COURSE! IF YOU'RE OKAY WITH JUST ME...
STEP
はた
CHEER
Hey!
YOU'RE CRUSH-ING ME!
DON'T JUST GO OFF INTO YER OWN WORLD WHEN I'M HERE!

HISS
ふしゅう～
Why'd Tomoyo have to go and be on day duty today?! I'm lonely!
IT REALLY IS ERIOL-KUN'S HOUSE...
SEEMS THAT WAY.
DING
ピ～ンポ～ン♪
DOOONG
HELLO?

E-EXCUSE ME. IT'S KINOMOTO.
AND DAIDOUJI.
BRZZ
LET ME OPEN IT FOR YOU!
OH!
COME ON IN!
C-COMING!
Oh ho ho
YER WALKIN' PRETTY WEIRD, SAKURA.
CRICK CRACK
ぎくしゃく
THANK YOU VERY MUCH FOR THE INVITATION.
BOW
Y-YES! THANK YOU!
I AM PLEASED YOU CAME!
SLIP

GOOD DAY.
WE ARE HONORED TO HAVE YOU AS GUESTS TODAY.
THIS IS KAITO-SAN.
HE HAS TAKEN CARE OF ME SINCE I WAS YOUNG. I HAVE BURDENED HIM IN MANY WAYS, I AM SURE.
YUNA D. KAITO.
PLEASED TO MAKE YOUR ACQUAINTANCE.
THANK YOU FOR BEING A FRIEND TO AKIHO-SAN.

AND YOU HAVE NEVER ONCE BEEN A BURDEN TO ME,
AKIHO-SAN.
JUMP
PLEASE, COME INSIDE.
BLUSH
WOW!

IT'S TOTALLY DIFFERENT FROM WHEN ERIOL-KUN LIVED HERE!
THAT SEEMS TO BE THE CASE.
WHAT A CUTE SITTING ROOM!
RATTLE カラ
カラ RATTLE
WHAT A PLEASANT AROMA!
THIS WAS A GIFT FROM OUR GUESTS. A TEA FLAVORED WITH SAKURA BLOSSOMS.
OH, THANK YOU!
TOMOYO-CHAN PICKED IT OUT.
SLIP
TICK TICK TICK
チッチッチ
CLINK
カチャ
コポポ
GLUB-UB-UB
HERE YOU ARE.

THANK YOU VERY MUCH!
IT'S GOOD!
THANK YOU. PLEASE TRY THIS AS WELL.
THANK YOU FOR THE FOOD!
ぱく
CHOMP
HANYAAAAN...
はっ
UH.

N-NO! I DIDN'T SAY ANYTHING!
じたばた FLAIL
じたばた FLAIL
WHAT'S THE MATTER?
かあぁ〜っ BLUSH
I SAID "HANYAAN" AGAIN...
IT'S VERY CUTE, THOUGH?
I WANTED TO TRY TO STOP SAYING IT, NOW THAT I'M IN MIDDLE SCHOOL... IT'S EMBARRASSING!
IT'S VERY TASTY!
WHERE WOULD ONE FIND SUCH A THING?
こくこく NOD NOD
I MADE IT.
OH!
SO IT'S HOMEMADE!

HE ALWAYS MAKES MY DINNERS, LUNCHES, AND SNACKS HIMSELF.
WOW! THAT'S DEDICA-TION!
NOT AT ALL.
THIS IS MY JOB, AFTER ALL.
AKIHO-CHAN...

CLAP
ぱっ
ONCE WE ARE DONE WITH OUR CAKE, I HAVE A PLACE TO SHOW YOU!
OH, WOW!

ARE ALL THESE BOOKS YOURS?!
THEY ARE. OR RATHER, THEY ARE THE BOOKS COLLECTED BY MY FAMILY.
YOURS MUST BE A FAMILY OF VORACIOUS READERS.
YES. THEY ALL LOVE BOOKS VERY MUCH.
WE COLLECT BOOKS FROM ALL OVER THE WORLD. THIS IS ONLY PART OF OUR COLLECTION.
I ALSO HAVE A STRONG LOVE OF BOOKS.
I CAME HERE TO JAPAN BECAUSE THERE WAS A CERTAIN BOOK I HAD TO HAVE.
WHA?
ALL THIS?
JUST BECAUSE OF A BOOK?

THAT WAS ONE REASON.
BUT ALSO...
THOOM
WHAT WAS THAT?
IS SOME-THING THE MAT-TER?
...

N–
NO! NOTHING!
OH! UM...
YOU SAID YOU WANTED TO SHOW ME ONE OF YOUR FAVORITE BOOKS, RIGHT?
YES!
I WOULD LOVE TO SEE IT.
OF COURSE!
STP
STP
I HAVE IT UP IN MY ROOM. I'LL BE RIGHT BACK.
STP
STP
STP
STP

DID SOME-THING HAPPEN?
GLANCE GLANCE
きょろきょろ
NO. I FELT IT.
SOME-WHERE AROUND HERE...
COULD IT BE...?
YEAH.
I THINK THERE'S A CARD HERE.
HUH?
ALL THESE BOOKS, BUT THIS SPOT...
...IS EMPTY?
IT CERTAINLY SEEMS SO.

VOLUMES ONE THROUGH NINE ARE HERE...
...BUT THE OTHER SIDE BEGINS AT 18.
SHING
I WONDER IF THEY'RE OUT AT A READING AREA?
HUH ?!
DID SOME-THING HAPPEN?
LOOK!
To be continued...

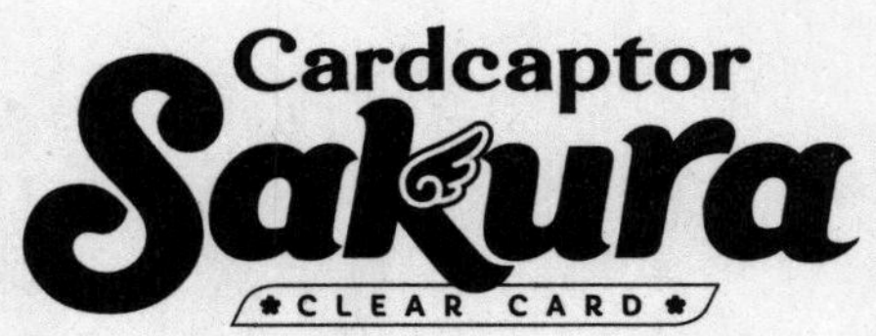
Cardcaptor
Sakura
CLEAR CARD

Cardcaptor
Sakura
CLEAR CARD

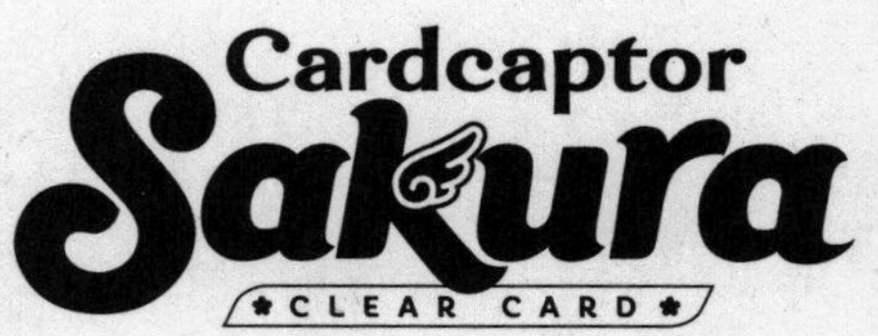
Cardcaptor
Sakura
CLEAR CARD

SLIDE
LOOK!
I'M PRETTY SURE...
SLIIIDE
...THE MISSING BOOKS ARE STILL HERE.
OH?
BUT THEY ARE INVISIBLE.
RUSTLE
Release!

Force without master! Heed the call of my Staff of Dreams and become my power!
Secure!
TING
CRACK
CRICK
CRICKLE
CRACKL

SNAP
FLASH
TWINKLE
I KNEW IT WAS A CARD!
TWINKLE
Lucid ...
LUCID
IT LOOKS LIKE THIS CARD HAS THE POWER TO TURN THINGS COMPLETELY INVISIBLE.
TURN
TOMOYO-CH-
ROLL
ONCE AGAIN, *I THOUGHT SOMETHING LIKE THIS MIGHT HAPPEN!*

I'M SO GLAD I HAVE MY PHONE WITH ME WHEREVER I GO!
WHAAAA?!
I'M A LITTLE WORRIED ABOUT TREMOR AND PICTURE QUALITY, BUT NECESSITY KNOWS NO BOUNDS!
SAKURA-CHAN! GIVE ME A POSE WITH THE CARD!
OH...
ERR... SURE...
OH!
I LEFT MY PHONE AND KERO-CHAN BEHIND...
I SEE...
WOOM
KERO-CHAN'S GONNA GET ALL SULKY WHEN HE LEARNS HE WASN'T AROUND DURING SOMETHING IMPORTANT AGAIN.
TAP
TIP
TAP

SORRY TO KEEP YOU WAITING!
TIP
TAP
FLUSTER
FLUSTER
...IS SOMETHING THE MATTER?
THIS BOOK IS-
THIS IS SUCH A MAGNIFICENT LIBRARY. I WAS WONDERING, MAY I TAKE SOME PHOTOS?
YES! OF COURSE.
THIS IS THE BOOK.
HUH? THERE'S NO TITLE?

THE BINDING DOES NOT LIST A TITLE, THAT'S TRUE.
THIS BOOK IS ENTITLED *ALICE IN CLOCKLAND.*
ALICE IN CLOCK-LAND?
LIKE *ALICE IN WONDER-LAND?*
THAT'S RIGHT.
IT HAS A DIFFERENT AUTHOR FROM THAT OF THE MORE FAMOUS *ALICE IN WONDERLAND* AND *THROUGH THE LOOKING-GLASS.*
BUT IT IS QUITE GOOD.

THE COVER IS SO BEAUTIFUL!
THE CLOCK MOTIF...
THIS CLOCK...
I FEEL LIKE I'VE SEEN IT BEFORE.
BUT WHERE?
SAKURA-SAN?

SORRY. I GOT CARRIED AWAY ADMIRING THE CRAFTSMANSHIP.
Eh heh
DELIGHT
ほんわ…
WHAT IS THE STORY ABOUT?
FLUTTER
I... CAN'T READ ANY OF IT.
IT'S NOT IN ENGLISH, EITHER. WHAT LANGUAGE IS IT?
I'M NOT SURE.
BUT I WAS TAUGHT TO READ IT...
...SO I UNDERSTAND MOST OF THE STORY.
YOU'RE REALLY TALENTED, AKIHO-CHAN!
OH, NO!
I'M NOT, REALLY.

COULD YOU TELL ME ABOUT THE STORY?
WELL ...
リリリン
BRING-RING-RING
リリリン♪
BRING-RING ♪
BRING-
カチャ
KA-CHAK
KAITO-SAN IS WONDERING IF WE WOULD LIKE SOMETHING COLD TO DRINK.
CAN WE HAVE DRINKS IN HERE?
コト
THIP
IF IT'S ALL RIGHT WITH YOU...

I'M HOME!
WELCOME BACK.
STP
ぱたぱた
STP
YOU'RE HOME EARLY.
OH, I SEE. FROM THE BAKERY?
I TOOK OFF WORK TODAY.
NAH. THE MOVERS.

WHAT'S FOR DINNER TONIGHT?
SLIIDE
すすす
FRIED RICE.
THAT SOUNDS REALLY GOOD!
CHEERY
うき
CHEERY
うき
LET ME GO CHANGE CLOTHES FIRST.
SAKURA.
YES?

... NEVER MIND.
WHA?
MIND IF I PUT *KONNYAKU* JELLY IN THE FRIED RICE?
YOU'D BETTER NOT!
BAM!
STOMP
STOMP
DO YOU HAVE TO TEASE ME ALL THE TIME?!
IT'S HAP-PENING AGAIN.

SLAM
SNOOZE
BY THE TIME WE RETURNED TO THE SITTING ROOM, KERO-CHAN WAS FAST ASLEEP.
Before we came, he was all "You'd better bring me in case anything happens!"
CRADLE
I'M HOME...
I'M REALLY LOOKING FORWARD...
...TO NEXT WEEKEND.

THE FOL-LOW-ING SUN-DAY

I'M GLAD THE WEATHER IS SO NICE TODAY!
OH!
I'D BETTER HURRY!
I WANT TO BE FIRST! I DON'T WANT HIM TO HAVE TO WAIT!
DAP
DAP
DAP
DAP.
SO BASICALLY ...
SAKURA'S OUT WITH THE BRAT.
AND YOU ARE NOT WITH HER?

Urgh...
WELL, TODAY SEEMS TA BE SOMETHIN' SPECIAL.
I EXPECTED SHE WOULD BE HAPPY TO HAVE YOU ALONG.
YEAH, THAT'S WHAT I THOUGHT TOO, BUT...
WE SHOULD LEAVE THEM ALONE FOR TODAY, KERO-CHAN.
WHY'S THAT?
IT'S PRIME FILMING TIME, AIN'T IT?
OH, I ASSURE YOU, I WOULD LOVE TO.
I WOULD ABSOLUTELY, POSITIVELY LOVE TO RECORD EVERY SECOND.
YOU'RE REALLY HANKERIN' TO, I CAN TELL!

BUT THOSE TWO HAVEN'T REALLY HAD A CHANCE TO BE ALONE IN QUITE SOME TIME.
WE WOULDN'T WANT TO INTERFERE WITH THEIR DATE.
HMM...
I GUESS SO. BUT WHAT IF SOMETHIN' WEIRD HAPPENS AGAIN?
LI-KUN WILL BE THERE TO HELP HER.
...SO WE DECIDED NOT TO GO.
I SEE.

WHAT I'M WONDERIN' IS WHY SPINNY AIN'T TAKING CALLS ANYMORE!
NOT LIKE HE'S GOT ANYTHIN' BETTER TO DO!
TAP
TAP
OH!
YUE! YOU EVER TRIED PLAYIN' ONLINE GAMES?
PSHOOO
AW, MAN!!

DASH
LI-KUN!
I'M SORRY FOR MAKING YOU WAIT!
NO, IT'S MY FAULT FOR COMING EARLY.
I WAS HERE 12 MINUTES BEFORE WE'D DECIDED TO MEET.
S-STILL! I FEEL BAD MAKING YOU WAIT FOR ME...

DON'T WORRY ABOUT IT.
LET'S GO.
LET'S!
STROLL
STROLL
WHAT IS IT?

OH, NOTHING!
Tomoeda Botanical Gardens
I DIDN'T KNOW THERE WAS A BOTANICAL GARDEN IN TOMOEDA.
WE WENT HERE ON A FIELD TRIP WHEN I WAS IN THE LOWER GRADES.
I HEARD YOU'D NEVER BEEN, SYAORAN-KUN!
HERE!
ARE YOU SURE?
MY DAD GOT THEM AT THE COLLEGE AND GAVE THEM TO ME.
HE TOLD ME TO USE THEM WITH SOMEONE SPECIAL.

SOMEONE SPECIAL...
BLUSH
わぁっ
BLUSH
かああっ
L-LET'S GO, THEN.
Y- YES, LET'S.
AWK-WARD
ぎくしゃく
THESE FLOWERS ARE ALL SO PRETTY!

RUSTLE
IT'S TRUE.
KA-POP
THAT'S IMPRES-SIVE.
IT LOOKS LIKE PUTTING THIS TOGETHER WAS A LOT OF WORK.

SHAKE
SHAKE
SHAKE
MAY I GO AHEAD AND EAT?
NOD
NOD
THANKS FOR THE FOOD.
SLIP
How is it? How is it?!

SHINE
ぱあっ
PRETTY GOOD!

RUSTLE
さわ

さわ
RUSTLE
さわ
RUSTLE
I WISH...
...THIS MOMENT COULD LAST FOREVER...

✿ To be continued... ✿

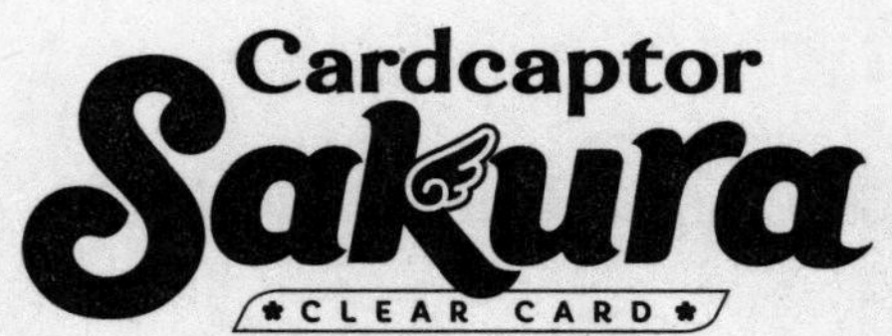
Cardcaptor
Sakura
CLEAR CARD

Cardcaptor
Sakura
CLEAR CARD

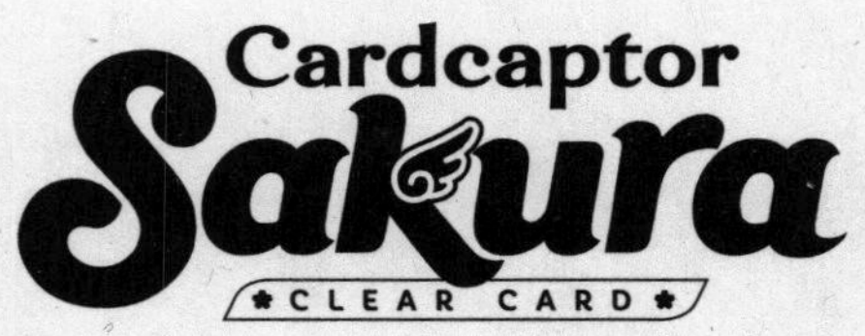
Cardcaptor
Sakura
CLEAR CARD

?!!
SHOOOOM
THIS IS...
THIS WIND ISN'T NATURAL.
YEAH. I'M SURE IT'S THE WORK OF A CARD.
THRUMM

Release!
FLASH
Secu–
...HUH?!
WHIRL
WHIRL
AAH!
WHIRL

SHOOOP
BAM
BAM
IT SEALED US IN?!
WHAT NOW ...?

CLAP
SHIIING
THWIP
Fuuka Shourai!
WHOOOSH

CRACK
GLOW
I THOUGHT THAT SPELL WOULDN'T WORK...
THOCK!
CLENCH
...
!

THWACK!
THOOOOM
HUH?!
SAKURA! MAKE IT A CARD!
R-RIGHT!

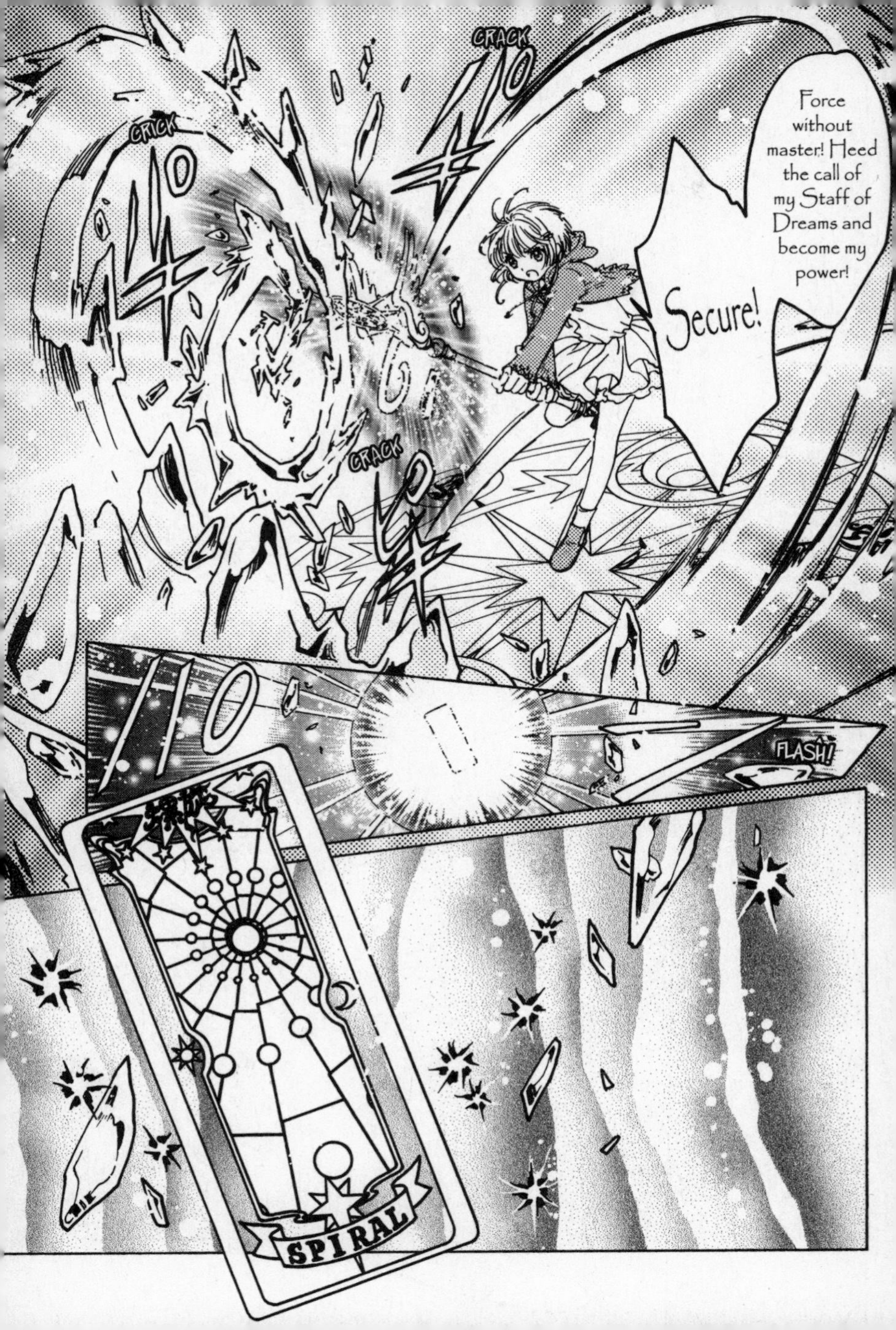
CRACK
CRICK
Force without master! Heed the call of my Staff of Dreams and become my power!
Secure!
CRACK
FLASH!
SPIRAL

DASH!
ARE YOU ALL RIGHT?!
YEAH ...
YOU SAVED ME, SYAORAN-KUN!
...
OH!

OUR LUNCH!
OH!
BAM!

HE ATE SOME OF IT THOUGH, RIGHT?
YEAH.
HE ATE SOME.
AND?
HE SAID IT WAS PRETTY GOOD.
FLOATY
IT'S TOO BAD ABOUT YOUR LUNCH...
...BUT THAT PART IS NICE, AT LEAST.
YOU CAN ALWAYS GO AN' MAKE IT AGAIN!
PAT
PAT
THAT'S RIGHT!
YEAH!
I'LL DO EVEN BETTER NEXT TIME!

I'M GOING TO HAVE TO START ON DINNER PRETTY SOON, TOO.
OH! SORRY TO DISTRACT YOU LIKE THIS!
NOT AT ALL!
MY DAD AND BROTHER WON'T BE HOME, SO IT'S JUST ME.
I CAN TAKE MY TIME MAKING WHATEVER I WANT.
LEAP
ぱっ
HEY! I'M HERE, TOO!
YOU CAN ALWAYS MAKE WHATEVER I WANT, CAN'T YOU?
Okay, fine!
I WISH I COULD COME OVER TO HELP...
TOMOYO-
YOU'RE GOING OUT WITH YOUR MOM TONIGHT, RIGHT?
DON'T WORRY ABOUT IT.
NEXT TIME, THEN.
NEXT TIME!
BYE FOR NOW!
BIP
ピ

BE-BEEP!
BE-BEEP!
AAH!
DING DOOONG
ピンポーン♪
BE RIGHT THERE!
THP
THP
HELLO!

WELCOME!
ARE YOU SURE IT'S OKAY FOR ME TO COME OVER THIS LATE?
OF COURSE!
COME ON IN!
SNIFF
SOME-THING SMELLS GOOD...
I WORKED HARD TO MAKE SOMETHING SINCE I KNEW YOU WERE COMING.
PLEASE EAT WITH ME!
YOU DIDN'T HAVE TO DO ALL THAT...
I'M HAPPY TO HAVE YOU OVER! IT'S KIND OF LONELY HAVING DINNER BY MYSELF!

THIS IS FROM KAITO-SAN!
HE SAID WE SHOULD ALL EAT IT TOGETHER!
WHAT ABOUT KAITO-SAN?
OH!
I TOLD HIM I WILL EAT HERE.
GRIP
THANK YOU!
DINNER'S ALMOST READY.
COULD YOU GIVE ME A HAND?
I'D LOVE TO!
DOES THIS LOOK OKAY?
KA-TOCK
ARE YOU OKAY WITH ONION, AKIHO-CHAN?
I LOVE ONION!
THAT'S GREAT!

ARE THERE ANY FOODS YOU DISLIKE?
NOT R-
OH!
WOBBLE
PURU
WOBBLE
PURU
I REALLY DON'T LIKE...
...KON-NYAKU JELLY.
ARE YOU SERI-OUS?!
NOTHING AGAINST KON-NYAKU, IT'S JUST...
...THAT TEXTURE...
GRAB
I KNOW EXACTLY WHAT YOU MEAN!
HUH?

I HATE KON-NYAKU!
わわわわ
GRIP
YOU, TOO?!
はわ
EUGHHHHHHHH
IT'S OKAY!
EVEN IF WE HATE KON-NYAKU...
...THERE ARE PLENTY OF PEOPLE WHO WILL EAT IT OFF OUR PLATES FOR US!
あああ...
OOH!
うん...
SURE...
FOR ME, MY BIG BROTHER...
NOW THAT YOU MENTION IT, KAITO-SAN LOVES KONNYAKU...
大丈夫かな。
I GUESS THAT'S FINE...

Yeah!
WE SHOULD BE JUST FINE!
YES!
I HOPE IT TURNED OUT OKAY...
WAS THAT REALLY THE PROB-LEM?!
THANKS FOR THE FOOD.
THANKS FOR THE FOOD.

CHOMP
ぱく
BA-DUM
どき
BA-DUM
どき
IT'S VERY GOOD!
SIGH
ほっ
I'M SO RELIEVED. I TRIED TO TASTE IT A BUNCH WHILE I WAS COOKING IT, BUT I WAS STILL A LITTLE ANXIOUS...
IT'S QUITE MILD...
...AND A LITTLE UNLIKE ANY BEEF STEW I'VE HAD DURING MY TRAVELS.
THAT MUST BE THE MISO I PUT IN.
OH! A SECRET INGREDI-ENT!
IT'S NOTHING AS GRAND AS ALL THAT. JUST A LITTLE TRICK MY BROTHER TAUGHT ME.
YOUR WHOLE FAMILY SEEMS QUITE WELL VERSED IN COOKING.
YEP!
WE TAKE TURNS FOR MEALS.

THEY DIDN'T LET ME USE COOKING OIL WHEN I WAS YOUNG,
BUT NOW THAT I'M IN MIDDLE SCHOOL I CAN!
YOU MEAN YOU MADE THIS, TOO?!
YEP!
I'M STILL LEARNING HOW TO DO IT.
Hee hee!
ぱくっ
CHOMP
It's quite good!
WHAT ABOUT THE PEOPLE IN YOUR FAMILY?
CAN THEY COOK?
WE'RE ALL SO BUSY ALL THE TIME...
WE HAVE TO DEPEND ON OTHERS FOR THAT KIND OF THING.
LIKE KAITO-SAN?
YES.

THAT'S STILL KIND OF IMPRES-SIVE...
Ehh...
SHAKE
SHAKE
IT'S NOT IMPRESSIVE!
I THINK YOU AND YOUR FAMILY, WHO CAN DO EVERYTHING ON YOUR OWN, ARE MUCH MORE IMPRESSIVE.
THAT'S NOT TRUE!
I'M ALWAYS BEING TAUGHT THINGS AND NEEDING HELP WITH THINGS!
IF IT'S NOT TOO MUCH TROUBLE, SAKURA-SAN...
...WOULD IT BE POSSIBLE FOR YOU TO TEACH ME HOW TO COOK, ALSO?
HUH ?!

FLUSTER
はわわっ
BUT... BUT...
I'M NOT REALLY THAT GOOD! I'M SURE IT'D BE EASIER TO LEARN FROM KAITO-SAN, WOULDN'T IT?!
I WANT TO TRY TO GET BETTER WITHOUT KAITO-SAN FINDING OUT.
OH!
IS IT THAT...
...YOU WANT TO TRY...
...TO COOK FOR KAITO-SAN?
かあああ
BLUSH
I KNOW WHAT THAT FEELS LIKE.

WANTING THE PERSON YOU LOVE TO EAT AND ENJOY FOOD YOU MADE FOR THEM...
...YES.
OKAY! LET'S BOTH GET BETTER!
BOTH?

I STILL HAVE A LONG WAY TO GO. LET'S BOTH TRY OUR BEST!
YEAH!
WOULD YOU LIKE SOME MORE STEW?
かたん
CLINK
I WOULD!
DRIFT
FLIT

ふわ
YAWN
コト
CLINK
OH, I'M SORRY!
Ah!
DID YOU HAVE TROUBLE SLEEPING?
??
I DON'T THINK SO...
とろん
DROWSY
HUH?
HUH...
AKIHO-CHAN!
!!
フワ
DRIFT

SLAM
PAP
WHAT THE-
...ER...
WHISPER
WHAT THE HECK HAPPENED?
WHISPER
SHE SUDDENLY FELL ASLEEP!
WHAT ?!
DRIFT

WHERE ?
THERE!
BAM!
FLIT
スイッ
SO YER SAYIN' THAT FUZZY THING UP THERE'S RESPONSIBLE FOR THE SURPRISE NAP?
I THINK SO.
IF I DON'T DEAL WITH IT, AKIHO-CHAN MIGHT BE STUCK SLEEPING FOREVER!
BETTER DO SOME-THIN' QUICK!

SET
I'M DEFINITELY GOING TO MAKE IT INTO A CARD.
HOLD ON UNTIL THEN, AKIHO-CHAN!
STAND
FLOAT
DASH!
HOLD IT!

DASH!
タタッ
FLIT
スイッ
DASH!
タッ
SLIP
キィ
CREAK
カターン
CLATTER
FLOAT

SHINE
Release!
I'M GOING TO CATCH YOU!
FLASH!
FLIGHT
Flight!

FLOAT
ふわ
NUZZLE
すり
NUZZLE
すり
HUH?
HUH?
WIGGLE
ピコ
WIGGLE
ピコ
SHE SEEMS REALLY HAPPY...
SHE'S TAKEN A LIKING TO YOU.

THANK YOU, FLIGHT-SAN.
BAM!
HERE I GO!
KERO-CHAN!
LEAP!
DO IT!

Continued in Volume 4